Andrew Oliver

Observations on the Use of Certain Prepositions in Petronius

With Special Reference to the Roman Sermo Plebius

Andrew Oliver

Observations on the Use of Certain Prepositions in Petronius
With Special Reference to the Roman Sermo Plebius

ISBN/EAN: 9783337019426

Printed in Europe, USA, Canada, Australia, Japan

Cover: Foto ©ninafisch / pixelio.de

More available books at **www.hansebooks.com**

OBSERVATIONS

ON

The Use of Certain Prepositions

IN

PETRONIUS

WITH SPECIAL REFERENCE TO THE

Roman

Sermo Plebeius

BY

ANDREW OLIVER, A. M. (Harv.), Ph. D.

INSTRUCTOR IN GREEK AND LATIN, ST. MATTHEW'S SCHOOL,
SAN MATEO, CALIFORNIA; FORMERLY OF THE POMFRET
SCHOOL, POMFRET, CONNECTICUT.

SAN FRANCISCO
1899

TABLE OF CONTENTS.

i

PART IV—THE PREPOSITION IN.

BIBLIOGRAPHY.

Anton, H. S., Studien zur Lateinischen Grammatik und
   Stilistik; Erfurt, 1869.

Bernhardy, G., Grundriss der Römischen Literatur; Halle,
   1872.

Bonnet, M., Le Latin de Grégoire de Tours; Paris, 1890.

Buechler, F., Petronii Satirae et Liber Priapeorum; Berlin, 1895.

Burmann, P., Titi Petronii Arbitri Satyricon Quae Super-
   sunt; Ed. II; Amsterdam, 1743.

Cesareo, I. A., De Petronii Sermone; Rome, 1887.

Diez, F., Grammaire des Langues Romanes; traduit par
   Alfred Morel-Fatio et Gaston Paris; Paris, 1876.

Draeger, A., Historische Syntax der Lateinischen Sprache;
   2 vols.; Leipsig, 1878–81.

Forcellini, A., Totius Latinitatis Lexicon[1]; 2 vols.; Padua,
   1771.

Friedländer, L., Petronii Cena Trimalchionis (Anmerk.);
   Leipsig, 1891.

Georges, K. E., Ausführliches Lateinisch-Deutsches Hand-
   wörterbuch; 2 vols.; Leipsig, 1869.

Goelzer, H., La Latinité de Saint Jérôme[2]; Paris, 1884.

de Guerle, Recherches Sceptiques sur le Satyricon et son
   Auteur; Paris, 1862.

von Guericke, A., De Linguae Vulgaris Reliquiis apud
   Petronium et in Scriptt. Pariet. Pompeianis; Königsberg, 1875.

Lindsay, W. M., The Latin Language; Oxford, 1894.

Krebs, J. P., Antibarbarus der Lateinischen Sprache;
   Frankfurt, 1876.

---

1 Also edited by Dr. F. Corradini; Padua, 1859-1878.
2 Cf. also "Grammaticae in Sulpicium Severum Observationes Potissimum ad Vul-
garem Latinum Sermonem Pertinentes," by the same author; [Paris, 1883.]

Ludwig, E., De Petronii Sermone Plebeio; Marburg, 1869.
Madvig, I. N., Latin Grammar, edited by Woods; Oxford, 1857.
Meyer-Lübke, W., Grammatik der Romanischen Sprachen; Leipsig, 1890–94.
Plew, J., De Diversitate Auctorum Historiae Augustae; Königsberg, 1859.
Rönsch, H., Itala und Vulgata; Marburg and Leipsig; 1875 and 1889.
Schmalz, J. G., Lateinische Syntax; in Iwan v. Müller's Handbuch der Classischen Altertumswissenschaft, Band II'; Nördlingen, 1885.
Schüssler, O., De Praepositionum AB, AD, EX, apud Ciceronem Usu; Hannover, 1880.
Segebade, J., Observationes Grammaticae et Criticae in Petronium; Halle, 1880.
Stinner, A., De Eo Quo Cicero in Epistolis Usus Est Sermone; Oppeln, 1879.
Stolz, F., Historische Grammatik der Lateinischen Sprache; Leipsig, 1894.
Studer; Rheinisches Museum für Philologie; herausgegeben von F. G. Welcker und F. Ritschl; Zweiter Jahrgang; Frankfurt am Main, 1843.
Teuffel, W. S., Geschicte der Römischen Literatur; Leipsig, 1890.
Wehle, Observationes Criticae in Petronium; Bonn, 1861.
Wölfflin, E., Bemerkungen über das Vulgärlatein; Archiv für Lateinischen Lexicographie; Leipsig, 1884–94.
Zumpt, K. G., Latin Grammar; translated by Schmitz; London, 1845.

INTRODUCTION.

Within the past twenty years a new interest, considerably
more far-reaching that that which had before existed among
scholars, has been aroused in what is commonly known as
the Roman "*Sermo Plebeius.*" Although the sources for such
study are moderately abundant in such specimens of Latin
as, for example, the language of the slaves in Plautus, to say
nothing of the statements occasionally found in Roman
grammarians, and in inscriptions of one sort or of another,
nevertheless, as far as the Roman novel is a factor, our data
are extremely limited in scope. In fact, there are but two
extant specimens[1] in Latin of genuine prose fiction. These
two are, accordingly, of peculiar interest; and with certain
grammatical features of one of them it is the purpose of
the present essay to deal.

Into any extended discussion of the much-mooted ques-
tion as to the exact limitations of the *Sermo Plebeius* it is
not my aim here to enter. A considerable mass of material
in that direction is accessible in the works of Bonnet, Sittl,
Wölfflin, Stolz, Miodonski, Cooper, and others, whose con-
clusions, though often conflicting, are of permanent interest
and value.

Nor is it my purpose to undertake a literary criticism of
the "Cena Trimalchionis," so remarkable for its touches of
keen wit, and for its many brilliant examples of repartee and
invective, as well as for its display of insight and unique
character delineation. On the other hand, what I have set
myself to do in the present instance is a task of a somewhat
different nature. My aim has been to collect and examine

---

1 The Satirae of Petronius, and the Metamorphoses of Apuleius.

2 Cf. Ott., Jahrb. 109, p. 763: "Ein sprechender Beweis hierfür ist uns die Cena
Trimalchionis des Petronius, dieses Kunstreiche Mosaikbild des campanischen
Dialekts."

as carefully as possible certain definite facts of syntax as exemplified in an unquestionably important literary specimen of plebeian Latin; namely, the fragmentary prose work of Petronius Arbiter. However long the original work of Petronius may have been, the extant fragments are from Books XV and XVI, a fact which suggests the probability that the author had at first written a book of considerable proportions.

Of the somewhat less than four thousand lines of literary material attributed to Petronius, there are more than five hundred in verse. The latter I have included in my general summary of the points under discussion, although it has seemed best at this time to omit any detailed treatment of the poetic element, as such.

But to proceed to the matter in hand. My paper consists of four parts, each part dealing with a single leading preposition, in its simple use. Verbs compounded with prepositions, although forming one of the marked characteristics of the *Sermo Plebeius*, as Wölfflin (Philol. 34, p. 157 f.) and Rönsch (Itala und Vulgata, p. 474) have already noted, I have thought it advisable to omit in the present paper. Moreover, the prepositions are classified by function throughout, and not as they occur in the order of the narrative. Idiomatic and adverbial expressions, except in some cases where the idiom does not appear to affect to any extent the inherent function of the preposition, I have grouped under distinct heads, a glance at which may be interesting and suggestive.

PART I—AD.

§1. The preposition AD is found in Petronius 237 times[1], and in at least a dozen different applications. Out of this number I find 104 cases in which this preposition is used with verbs of motion, or in which the idea of motion is directly involved. This use of AD is in most instances so clearly marked and is so well known that little need be said of it beyond the citation of the passages in which it occurs. Doubtful cases I have treated separately in another part of this discussion.

The following are the passages in which this use of AD is employed: §§1,3; 1,5; 2,10; 2,14; 4,4; 8,4; 10,5; 10,13; 13,5; 13,12; 15,13; 16,9; 17,22; 22,14; 22,19; 136,21[2]; 37,1; 62,3; 22,21; 24,10; 24,14; 25,1; 26,11; 27,5. 28,2; 35,15; 36,2; 36,11; 40,21; 41,19; 42,10; 46,5; 52,16; 137,37; 49,15; 97,20; 52,25; 60,12; 61,20; 63,18; 64,25; 68,17; 69,14; 73,3; 74,14; 74,24; 74,26; 75,16; 75,20; 78,11; 79,10; 140,4; 62,15; 81,13; 82,5; 82,12; 87,2; 89,45[2]; 89,50[2]; 90,4; 94,41; 100,3; 101,32; 98,18; 98,50; 103,9; 105,19; 105,24; 33,13; 72,13; 106,13; 107,31; 108,27; 109,23; 111,34; 112,12; 113,28; 114,2; 114,10; 114,28; 115,14; 116,11; 116,13; 117,6; 118,4; 28,14; 86,9; 118,5; 118,15; 120,87[2]; 121,121[2]; 122,147[2]; 124,272[2]; 127,10; 130,7; 132,1; 132,1; 132,27[2]; 133,19[2]; 133,20[2]; 134,15; 136,11; 30,1; 89,36[2].

§2. My next consideration is that of AD in cases where physical motion is neither directly expressed nor necessarily implied, although frequently in such instances the verb in itself is one of motion. These cases for the most part speak for themselves[3], and I append a list as follows:

---

[1] Exclusive of compounds.

[2] The passages marked 2 are found in the poetic fragments. All references, unless otherwise specified, are to Bücheler's Third Edition (Berlin, 1895.)

[3] With the exception of the plebeian tendency, in some of these instances, to exaggerate the use of the preposition, there is here nothing abnormal or unclassical.

Ad hanc aetatem perveni, §§25,15; Ad nos respexit, 48,3; Ad quem respiciens, 52,8; Respiciens ad mensam, 60,9; Ad Nicerotem respexit, 61,2; Ut respexi ad comitem, 62,7; Ad delicias suas respexit, 64,14; Respiciens ad familiam, 74,13; Ad parentalia invitatos, 78,9; Si ad eloquentiam pervenisset, 88,21; Eumolpus convertit ad novitatem rei mentem, 117,1; Respiciens ad Eumolpon, 96,13; Ad ordinem tristitiae redimus, 103, 17; Ad inguina mea luminibus deflexis, 105,26; Ad unicum fugitivi argumentum pervenerit, 105,31; Revocatae ad pacem manus, 109,2; Rediit ad carmina sua, 109,28; Mentes ad sanitatem revocantur, 111,30; Ad summos honores perveniunt, 116,19; Quirites ad praedam..suffragia vertunt, 119,40; Ad ultimam tristitiam perductus, 24,2; "Forsitan rediret hoc corpus ad vires," 138,19; "..Invitare ad pigiciaca sacra," 140,14; "Fortuna communis coepit redire ad paenitentiam," 141,3; "Ad temeritatem confugimus," (or, as one might say: "We made a bold stroke;") 102,2.

§3, The use of AD in the adverbial expression "*Ad summam*" has been observed to occur more frequently in Petronius than in other authors[1]; and it is, moreover, characteristic of a class of formulas which seem to have been employed only in the talk of the household[2] (*Sermo Familiaris*). This fact is confirmed by various passages in which the words are found in other Latin writers. In Petronius I find the expression used fourteen times; ten times in the conversation of the freedmen, and four times in the other parts of the story. Furthermore, in the latter case it appears always to be found only in those passages in which the hero Encolpius either reports his own words[3] or the words of another; it is not found in his own narrative pure and simple. The expression is still further observed by Segebade[2] to occur most frequently in instances where, after an enumeration of some circumstances, the speech passes over to the most important item of all, to which a special emphasis is thus given. Examples of this use are

[1] Cf. Studer, p. 87, Bücheler; Symb. Philol. Bonnet, p. 61.
[2] See Segebade, "Observationes in Petronium," p. 11.
[3] Cf. §2, 16.

clearly seen in §§37,16; 45,34; 58,21; 71,4; 134,20; 140,8.
A somewhat more marked use of this formula is found in
§§38,4; 57,9; and 105,11. In these cases the enumeration
of items or facts by the speaker is intended rather to follow
than precede. In the other passages in Petronius in which
the words occur, neither of the foregoing uses is altogether
apparent and clearly defined. The citations are as follows:
§§2,16; 31,5; 75,21; 77,13. In the first one of these three
passages, the attention of the reader is called by" *Ad
summam*" to the designation of a notable circumstance,
the expression thus running:

"Eloquentia stetit et obmutuit. Ad summam, quis postea
Thucydidis, quis Hyperidis ad famam processit?"¹

Other passages illustrating this use with greater or less
emphasis are §§37,16; 31,5²; 57,27; 75,21; and 77,13. So
much for "*Ad summam*" in this survey. Suffice it to add
that the expression occurs nowhere in the poetic fragments.

§4. Turning now to the matter of syntax development
in Petronius at the expense of inflectional forms, a marked
feature of the *Sermo Plebeius*, we find in a number of
instances the prepositions AD, DE, and CUM taking the place
of the ordinary case-constructions in Ciceronian Latin. A
treatment of DE and CUM in this connection will be found
in another part of this paper, while I wish here to call
attention to some instances where AD with the Accusative
appears to be used instead of the simple Dative of classic
Latin:

"Ad neutram partem adsensionem flectentibus," §§17,1;
"Aquam poposcit ad manus," 27,17; "Qui omnia ad se
fecerunt," 38,23; "Dispensatorem ad bestias³ dedit," 45,18.

The verb "Defero" in classic writers is common enough
either with the simple Dative of the Indirect Object, or with

---

1 I have followed the reading of Haase—Misc. Philol. III, p 16 [1861], and Bücheler, the former of whom, Segebade declares, (p. 11) is justified in making the transposition from the reading of the earlier MS., which is: "qui postea ad summam Thucydidis."

2 In §31 Bücheler has, with some hesitation, advised that the formula as here found should be added to the words of the slave. Segebade, moreover, concurs in this opinion.

3 Cf., however, the remarks on this passage on p. 5 of this paper.

AD and the Accusative. Petronius, however, seems invariably to prefer the latter use, e.g.:

"Nec amoris arbitrium ad alium judicem detuli," §§91,19;
"....Quas etiam ad immeritos deferre gratia solet," 83,24;
"Si....indicium ad amicos detulerit," 125,11.

§5. There are four instances in which AD appears to have the same function as that rather frequently assumed by the Greek κατά with the Accusative, and occasionally by πρός:

"....caryotas ad numerum divisere cenantibus," §§40,22; "Quotidie me solebam ad illum (sc. candelabrum) metiri'," 75,22; "Extremitates imaginum erant ad similitudinem praecisae," 83,6; "....hominis vestigium ad corporis mei mensuram figuravi," 97,15.

§6. The omission of certain prepositions in plebeian Latin has been shown by Von Guericke[2] to be not infrequent. In Petronius I have found three instances, two of which Von Guericke has also observed, in which AD is omitted where in Ciceronian Latin we should certainly expect to find it expressed. In the first of the following cases the words are uttered by the hero, Encolpius; in the second, by the rag-dealer, Echion; and in the third, by the "parvenu" Trimalchio:

(1) Accedo aniculam, §§6,9; (2) Africam ire, 48,8; [the omission of either AD or IN] (3) Admissus Caesarem, 51,3.

In reference to the latter passage Ludwig[3] says: "Non dubium est quin illa dictio quae praeclare Trimalchionem decet in ceteris ejus vitiis collocanda." Cf. "Thessaliam pervenire," Apul. Met., i,24; also "Missus Germaniam superiorem translatus est," Spart. Hadr. 2,5; and "Asiam venit'," Gall. 2,5.

---

1 Forcellini gives a single passage fr. Juvenal 6, 358: "Nec se metitur ad illum"; classic usage throughout presenting the standard of measurement iu Abl. (i. e., w. metior).

2 De Liuguae Vulgaris Reliquiis, etc., pp. 54-55.

3 De Petronii Sermone Plebeio, p. 34.

4 This form of usage has been regarded as a type of the "Sermo Rusticus." See Ludwig et al. Cf., however, the occasional occurrence of this form of usage iu classic writers; e. g. Caesar, Bell. Gall., III, 7: "Illyricum profectus;" Id., Bell Civ III, 41: "Macedoniam pervenit;" Liv. X, 37: "Etruriam transducto exercitu;" Id. XXX, 24: "Africam transiturus;" etc. Zumpt (Lat. Gram.) p. 302, observes that this construction is rare iu the earlier writers, but becomes somewhat more frequent in the later ones.

Moreover, in Plautus there are a number of instances of the omission¹ of prepositions, though in Terence this construction is very rare; e. g.: Plaut. Curc. 206, 339: "Ire Acheruntem;" Plaut. Poen. IV, 2, 9: "Ire Cariam;" Terence, Eun. 536: "Malam rem hinc ibis;" Plaut. Trin. 639: "Officio migrare" [AB omitted]; Plaut. Men. 134: "Salute" [CUM omitted]; Plaut. Rud. 910: [CUM omitted]; Plaut. Merc. 824: [CUM omitted]; Plaut. Trin. 265: "Saxo salire" [DE omitted]; etc.

§7. The use of AD in the sense of APUD, and vice versa, has been admirably treated by Rönsch², who cites many examples from vulgar and late Latin, curiously introducing the passage from Petronius, §45,20, which, I think, however, need not necessarily be thus classified. In fact, Rönsch has apparently misquoted this passage in referring to it as "AD bestias pugnare," although the sense may perhaps be contained in these words. Both Bücheler and Friedländer³, following the MSS., read "Dispensatorem AD bestias dedit," and make no allusion in their critical apparatus to any other proposed reading. In the light of the context, what Rönsch undoubtedly means, and with reason, I think, is that the slave Glyco (the grammatical subject of "dedit") could not, upon his own responsibility, give the steward (dispensator) to the beasts; he would rather be obliged to hand him over to the master (Titus noster), who would then "pit him with" the beasts. Although this use of AD is most frequent in plebeian and in late Latin, it is by no means wanting in classic prose.⁴ Plautus, moreover, has a number of interesting examples; e. g. Capt. Prol. 49: "Ad patrem manere"; Id. Capt. 695, and Aul. III, 2, 25: "Ad patrem esse"; Id. Asin. 825: "Ad amicum potare"; also Ter. Heauton. 979: "Ad sororem esse"; etc. Cf. also, in late usage, Turp. 172: "Mansiones ad amicam"; and Spartian. Hadr. 13; Sever.

---

1 Due allowance must, of course, be made for metrical considerations.
2 Itala und Vulgata, pp. 39c-392.
3 See Micheler (Ed. III) p. 30; also Friedländer, p. 112.
4 E. g. Cic. Att. X, 4: "Fuit AD me sane diu," etc.

3,8. Pescenn. 5; Capitol. Anton. P.7; Anton. Phil. 27; Pertin. 3; Clod. Alb. 6; Opil. Macr. 4; Gordian. 5; etc.

§8. The fondness of Petronius for the combination USQUE AD carrying with it, as in other writers, the idea of extent, is a marked feature not only of the *Cena Trimalchionis*, but also of the other portions of the narrative. There are twelve[1] cases, as follows:

".... non potuerunt usque ad senectutem canescere,"§§2,19; ".... fruorque votis usque ad invidiam felicibus," 11,3; ".... manibus usque ad articulorum strepitum constrictis," 17,6; ".... qui me usque ad necessitatem mortis deducit," 17,19; "Ascyltos cum.... usque ad lacrimas rideret," 57,2; ".... usque ad os molestus umor accidere (sc. coepit),"60,16; ".... diduxit usque ad cameram os ebrium," 73,10; ".... mutemus colores a capillis usque ad ungues," 102,37; ".... quae.... usque ad furorem averteretur," 110,18; "Supercilia usque ad malarum scripturam currentia," 126,34; "... ante hunc diem usque ad mortem deliqui," 130,3; ".... usque ad satietatem osculis fruor," 131,32.

In addition to the foregoing cases of this usage I find two instances where AD is used without USQUE, yet where practically the same sense seems to be contained: §§2,17: ".... quis Hyperidis ad famam processit?" 71,11: ".... totum a primo ad ultimum ingenescente familia recitavit." In either of these examples Petronius might have employed USQUE with entire consistency, and we should not have been surprised had he done so.

§9. The use of AD suggesting the notion of consequence or effect I have observed in the following eight passages:

§§14,21: "Cociones qui ad clamorem confluxerant"; 27,15: "Ad quod signum matellam spado.... subjecit"; 41,14: "Ad quem sonum conversus Trimalchio," etc.; 45,34: "Thraex, qui et ipse ad[2] dictata pugnavit"; 86,4: "Ad hoc votum ephebus ultro se admovit"; 103,14:

---

1 I have found one instance of "USQUE IN" in the same sense, viz., 2,13,3: "USQUE IN injuriam vigilavit?" Possibly in this instance, as Professor Sihler of New York has suggested, the occurrence of the preposition may be owing to dittography.

2 In the light of the context in this passage, I believe the meaning to be that even [et] the gladiator fought only as he was urged on by the spectators. The meaning, however, may be that he fought accompanied by words which he himself uttered. But in either case the force of the preposition would be unaltered.

"Notavit sibi ad lunam tonsorem intempestivo inhaerentem ministerio"; 104,12: "Illi qui sunt, qui nocte ad lunam. radebantur," etc.; 98,15: "Ad quem motum Eumolpus conversus," etc.

§10. The tendency in ante-Hadrian Latin, as in the later form of the language, to extend the use of many of the prepositions, is in a number of instances rather strongly marked in Petronius, and is referred to from time to time in this paper. Let us now turn again to AD and briefly survey the cases in which this preposition is employed conveying merely the idea of proximity. I have classified these as follows:

§§14,12: "Nihil ad manum erat"; 29,2: "Ad sinistram enim....canis ingens, catena vinctus, in pariete erat pictus," etc.; 44,10: "Tunc habitabat ad arcum veterem....piper"; 46,9: "Habebis ad latus servulum"; 49,8: "Cum constitisset ad mensam cocus tristis"; 58,1: "Giton, qui ad pedes stabat, risum....effudit"; 61,18: "Huius contubernalis ad villam[1] supremum diem obiit"; 64,12: "Appositaque ad os manu nescio quid taetrum exsibilavit"; 64,36: "Trimalchio.... jussit potiones dividi omnibus servis, qui ad pedes sedebant", etc.; 70,10: "....qui rixam ad lacum fecissent"; 71,30: "Ad dexteram meam ponas statuam Fortunatae meae", etc.; 77,14: "Et habet ad mare paternum hospitium"; 83,22: "Is ergo ad latus constitit meum"; 94,30: "Et iam semicinctio lecti stantis ad parietem spondam vinxeram", etc.

§11. Examples of the Gerundive construction with AD are be no means wanting in Petronius; and in all I have found eight cases of this usage:

"Ad scindendum aprum non ille Carpus accessit", §§40,13;
"....Capuam exierat ad scita expedienda", 62,1;
"Intorto....pallio composui ad proeliandum gradum", 80,7; "....Contentus....annis ad patiendum gestientibus", 87,15; } Simple Gerund.
"Procurrere piscatores....ad praedam rapiendam", 114,36;

---

[1] Cf. a similar use of "Ad villam" in Plin. Ep. II, 2, 3. For remarks on the use of AD in the sense of APUD, see p. 5 et sq.

N. B. A curious and, I think, unique use of AD occurs in §109,17: "Epulae ad certamen prolatae." In this passage "AD certamen" appears to be used similarly to the adverb "certatim" in meaning, although, as Kelly has remarked ["Propertius Petronius," etc., London, 1854] (p. 311, Note), some of the English and the French translators have understood the words "Ad certamen" to mean "to the field of battle." But I believe the latter to be a misconstruction of the thought and sense.

8.

"Oculos ad arcessendos sensus longius mittit", 115,45;
."Ad reficiendum ignem in viciniam cucurrit", 136,9; "In
templum ire ad vota nucupanda", 140,12.

PART II—CUM.

§12. The use of this preposition in its simple form in
Petronius is confined to eighty-six cases, in seventeen of
which I find the word employed in its simplest classic[1] sense:
§§14,15; 16,6; 22,11; 28,13; 30,3; 31,22; 33,9; 49,22;
51,3; 56,17; 56,21; 97,2; 97,16; 99,18; 117,40; 136,32;
137,11.

In addition to these cases there occurs one instance[2] of
this usage in the poetry of Petronius, and here it is interesting to note that the preposition falls between the noun and
its adjective. Moreover, I find only three[3] parallels to this
order of words throughout the work, and these are confined
exclusively to the poetic passages.

§13. A single instance in which CUM is undoubtedly
used as in Terence, Eun.[1] 4,3,9, and occasionally elsewhere
in classic writers, appears in Petronius, §90,6, where the
hero Encolpius, in a moment of utter displeasure says to
the frightened Eumolpus: "Quid tibi vis cum isto morbo?"
or as we might say in the vernacular: "What do you mean
by this cursed disease of yours?" The tone is obviously
one of disparagement.

§14. To proceed further with our inquiry, by way of
comparison with classical usage, into Petronius' use of CUM,
it is worth while to consider the passages in which this
preposition is used, as in Caesar[5] and Cicero,[6] to designate

---

1 E. g. "Vixi cum Pansa in Pompeiano." Cic.

2 In the mock-heroic passage, §123,238.

3 §§122,153, "Summo de vertice"; 123,203, "Magnam in hastam"; 127,27, "Idaeo de
vertice". This position of the preposition is not uncommon in Cic. and the best classical writers. E. g. Cic. Brut. §79 (fin.); Id. Inv. 1,28,41; 2,11,37; et al.

4 "......in' hinc, quo dignus, cum donis tuis tam lepidis."

5 E. g. B. G. I,20: "Multis cum lacrimis aliquem obsecrare."

6 Verr. 2,1,24, §63: "Cum magna calamitate et prope pernicie civitatis."

the circumstances, manner,[1] or relations with which an act
is connected, or by which it is accompanied. The classical
and the plebeian forms of expression are, in this usage,
essentially identical.

§§29,7: "Venalicium cum[2] titulis pictum"; 31,16: "Asellus
erat Corinthius cum bisaccio positus"; 33,4: "Sequebatur
puer cum tabula terebinthina"; 34,9: "Intraverunt duo
Aethiopes....cum pusillis utribus"; 40,4: "In quibus....
erant (sc. picti) subsessores cum venabulis"; 40,17: "Parati
aucupes cum harundinibus fuerunt"; 49,1: "Repositorium
cum sue ingenti mensam occupavit"; 53,15: "....quibus
Trimalchio cum elogio exheredabatur" 54,8: "Fortunata
crinibus passis cum scypho...proclamavit"; 60,10: "Repositorium cum[3] placentis aliquot erat positum"; 65;12:
"Habinnam...cum admiratione ingenti spectabam"; 99,17:
"Eumolpus...mercennarium...exire cum sarcinis jubet";
114,19: "....cum clamore flevi"; 122,155 (poetry): "Inten-
tans cum voce manus ad sidera dixit"; 137,33: "Nuces cum
precatione mersit in vinum"; 138,12: "Chrysis....cum
periculo capitis persequi destinat"; 92,18: "Frequentia
ingens circumvenit cum plausu et admiratione."

§15. The attributive use of CUM with a substantive, as
in Livy[4] II, 52,7, and elsewhere in the classic writers, I have
found in Petronius in the three passages which follow:

§§28,14: "In cuius poste libellus erat cum hac inscrip-
tione fixus"; 34,16: "Quarum in cervicibus pittacia erant
affixa cum hoc titulo"; 35,12: "Caespes cum herbis excisus
favum sustinebat."

§16. The ordinary instrumental ablative in classic usage
appears in Petronius, in one or two instances, to give way
to the prepositional form of expression, which in this connection has been observed by the grammarians to be confined mainly to the ante-classical, the poetic, or the scientific

1 There are some cases where the Ciceronian Ablative of Instrument or Means is
supplanted in Petronius by CUM with the Abl. These instances will be found in
another part of this discussion.

2 In this passage CUM is wanting in the MSS. See Bücheler (Tert. Ed., Berlin,
1895), p. 20.

3 The usage in Petr.,§1,10, may be included in this list, rather than in the pregnant
sense, to which I have called attention in another part of this paper: "Piratas cum
catenis in litore stantes," etc.

4 "......et huic proelium cum Tuscis ad Janiculum erat crimini."

writers[1]. But even in these cases, I think, the simple notion of attendance or accompaniment is often somewhat distinctly felt, as in the second of these examples:

(1) "Aggrediuntur nos furentes nautae cum funibus", §105,15; (2) "Infecta materies ibat cum fluctibus", §114,35.

N. B. In reference to the late use of CUM with the Ablative in place of the Ablative of Instrument, so called, Bonnet has an interesting passage in his "La Latinité de Grégoire de Tours[2]," as follows:

"Parmi les fonctions que cette préposition remplit, il en est deux surtout qui ont de l'importance. C'est d' abord CUM avec l'ablatif remplaçant l'ablatif instrumental d'une manière plus général qu' à l'epoque classique; puis CUM joint aux noms des personnes, de façon à se rapprocher beaucoup de APUD, sans qu' on puisse dire cependant que l'un soit mis à dessein pour l'autre", etc.

Moreover, P. Geyer in a suggestive article[3] on this subject, observes: "Les Gaulois emploient volontiers APUD pour CUM"; and Bonnet[4] adds: "Mais cela n'arrive pas à Grégoire."

N. B. The use of CUM as in Cicero, De Orat., 1,2,8: "....hanc rationem dicendi cum imperatoris laude comparare", does not appear in Petronius.

§17. Petronius' employment of CUM, as in a familiar passage from Caesar,[5] implying connection, agreement, or union between two objects, is seen in the words which I quote from §94,12: "Raram fecit mixturam cum sapientiâ forma", an exact parallel to which I do not find elsewhere in this author. Moreover, the use of CUM conveying the idea of an intimate association or companionship, at times coupled, as in §44,20, with that of sharing some object with another, is rather marked in Petronius, and is of course com-

[1] E. g. Lucil. ap. Non. p. 261,6: "acribus inter se cum armis confligere." Cf. also Claud. Quadrig. ap. Gell. 9,13.10, etc.

[2] p. 603.

[3] Archiv f. Lat. Lex. II, p. 25 et sq.

[4] Ibid.

[5] "Cum veteribus copiis se conjungere", Bell. Gall. I., 37.

mon enough in Ciceronian' usage. The passages are self-explanatory:

"Aediles.... qui cum pistoribus colludunt", §§44,5: "Amicus.... cum quo audacter posses in tenebris micare", 44,12; "Panem.... non potuisses cum altero devorare", 44,20; "Cum vicensimariis magnam mantissam habet", 65,21; "Intrat Eumolpus cum Gitone", 94,31; "Doctores.... qui necesse habent cum insanientibus furere", 3,6; "Sic dividere cum fratre nolito", 11,10; "Rusticus.... cum muliercula comite propius accessit", 12,8; "Quae.... cum Quartilla in cellam venerat nostram", 25,6; "Nam et infans cum paribus inclinata sum", 25,13; "Filiamque.... cum fratre ephebo .... reliquit", 140,11; "Ut veterem cum Gitone meo rationem reducerem", 10,18; "Videor mihi cum² illo loqui", 42,6; "Dum Eumolpus cum² Bargate in secreto loquitur", 97,1; "Quod.... cum³ ea parte corporis verba contulerim", 132,40; "Nihil est commodius quam semper cum² sapientia loqui", 140,41.

§18. Turning to the use of CUM in expressions involving the idea of strife' or difference, we meet with six characteristic passages, which I have thus tabulated:

§§9,17: "Cum.... muliere pugnasti"; 19,13: (1) "Ut .... ipse cum Quartilla consisterem; 19,14: (2) Ascyltus cum ancilla; 19,14: (3) Giton cum virgine"; [sc. "si depugnandum foret."] 105,1: "Nisi cum pelago ventus irascitur"; 132,46: "Quid? non et Ulixes cum corde litigat suo?"

§19. In spite of the fondness of Petronius for an excessive⁵ use of prepositions, from the classical⁶ point of view, the occurrence of CUM in a pregnant sense is with this author comparatively rare. I have noted the following expressions of this idea:

---

1 E. g. Cic. Off. I, 17,51: "Nulla (sc. societas) cavior quam ea quae cum republica est unicuique nostrum", etc., etc.

2 This use in §42,6 is like Caesar's "cum aliquo agere", B. G. I., 13; and elsewhere, as in Cic. de Or. 1,13,57: "Haec ego cum ipsis philosophis disserebam."

3 A curious phrase—I find no parallel in classical usage.

4 Cf. Caesar, B. G. I., 1: "......quibuscum continenter bellum gerunt"; Val-Max. 4,1,12: "cum Scipione dissentire", etc.

5 I have tabulated more than 500 instances of the preposition IN; q. v.

6 Cf. Cic. Verr. Actio I, 8,22: "......fiscos cum pecunia Siciliensi"; also Id. Tusc. Disp. 5,23,65: "Immissi cum falcibus"; et Id Att. 6,9: "Te Romam venisse cum febri"; et Liv. 30,24: "Onerariae naves cum commeatu", etc. This usage is found all the way from a fragment of Eunius quoted by Cic. De Sen. I, 1 ["Ille vir hand magna cum re, sed plenu' fidei"] down to the time of Suetonius (e. g. Tib. 3(?), and later.

§§28,10: "Symphoniacus cum minimis tibiis accessit"; 95,1: "Deversitor cum parte cenulae intervenit"; 114,17: "Tryphaenam....scaphae impositam cum maxima sarcinarum parte," etc ; 141,1: "Navis....cum pecunia tua et familia non venit".

§20. In conclusion, it may be well to glance at the single instance which I have found of the use of this preposition with the adjective "Aequalis," describing the relation of two subjects to a common object. In Cicero we find "Idem" in this construction, which, by the way, never has reference to the identity[1] of two subjects, as the lexicographers have observed. In this connection cf. Cic. de Or. 2,33, 144: "Tibi mecum in eodem est pistrino vivendum", et al. The passage to which I refer in Petronius is in §108,4: "Et deformis praeter spoliati capitis dedecus superciliorum etiam aequalis cum fronte calvities."

§21. Lastly, the anastrophical occurrence of CUM, marked solely by its use as enclitic to the personal pronouns of the 1st and 3d Pers. Sing., and of the 1st and 2d Pers. Plu., is seen in the following eleven instances:

MECUM: §§62,3; 99,3; 76,26; 87,5; 109,25.

SECUM[2] (Sing. only): §§43,20; 43,25.

NOBISCUM: §101,12.

VOBISCUM: §§16,9; 18,10.

─────────

PART III—DE.

§22. Having now made some examination into the uses of AD and CUM in Petronius, let us pass to a consideration of the preposition DE as it is found in this author. In the first place, of the total number of passages in which the word occurs, about one seventh are instances of its use as in

─────────

1 Cf. Krebs, Antibarb. p. 538.

2 SECUM occurs once in the poetry: §123,231; and here, as in the other instances, in the Singular. TECUM and QUIBUSCUM I do not find in this author.

It is interesting to compare Bonnet's statement (La Latinité de Grégoire de Tours, p. 603): "Grégoire dit mecum, tecum, etc., mais non quibus um."

Caes. B. G. I., 31,10: "....De altera parte agri Sequanos decedere juberet"; i. e. in its simplest sense with verbs of motion. I have collated the examples of this usage as follows: §§9,15; 38,25'; 41,23; 56,12; 58,25; 59,2'; 92,13 (bis); 95,11; 117,20; 134,21.

§23. A slightly different and somewhat more frequent use of DE in Petronius is to indicate the person or place from which something is removed or taken, whether this be material or ideal[2]: §§11,9; 18,4; 20,9; 37,6; 43,4; 45,35; 46,10; 51,6; 69,10; 73,13; 74,28; 76,20[3]; 95,19; 110,4; 131,8; 135,11. In these passages the plebeian usage is essentially in accord with the Ciceronian, and seems to call for no special comment.

§24. The next usage in the order of frequent occurrence in Petronius is that of DE introducing the material of which a thing is made, there being thirteen cases, viz.:

"Videt manuciolum de stramentis factum", §§63,19; "Habuimus...et panem autopyrum de[4] suo sibi...", 66,6; "Quicquid videtis....de uno corpore est factum", 69,24; "Omnia ista de fimo[5] facta sunt aut certe de luto", 69,26; "Ista cocus meus de porco fecit", 70,2; "Volueris, de vulva faciet piscem", 70,3; "De lardo palumbum, de perna turturem, de colaepio gallinam (sc. faciet cocus meus)", 70,4; "Qui de porco anserem fecerat", 70,29; "De una die duas facere, nihil malo", 72,8; "Qui paulo ante de porco aves piscesque fecerat", 74,10; "Ne viderer de nave carcerem facere", 105,7.

---

1 In this passage the phrase DE MEDIO is used in a somewhat idiomatic way, although the force of the preposition is in no sense abnormal.

Note: In §38,25 the phrase is: "Amici de medio," i. e., as we should say, "Good bye to friends." In §59,2 we read: "Scordalias de medio," an expression, as the context shows, uttered in a moment of excitement by the parvenu Trimalchio, to the effect that there shall be "NO MORE wrangling."

2 Cf. Cic. de Orat. 3,33,133: "Hoc audivi de patre", etc.

3 In §76,20 occurs the expression "MANUM DE TABULA," which Friedländer (p. 317, Anmerk.) compares with Cic. Fam. VII, 25: "Sed heus tu, manum de tabula, magister citius adest quam putaramus"; and Pliu. XXV, 80: "Quod scilicet manum de tabula sciret tollere."

4 Cf. the passages from Cicero, cited by Friedländer, p. 298, Anmerkungen (Petr. Cena Trimal., Leipsig, 1891): "Ueber diese der lateinischen Volkssprache eigne Verbindung (auch bei Cic. Verr. 2,82, Phil. 2,96, Att. VII, 11,1) vgl. Reisig-Haase, Anm. 387 (Ausg. v. Schmalz u. Landgraf III, 142 f.).

5 I have here followed the standard text of Bücheler's 3d edition. The MSS. read "DEFACTA" and "DEFUNCTA" respectively, the latter reading being in H [Codex Traguriensis] Cf. Bücheler, p. 47; also Friedländer, Petr. Cen. Trim., p. 172.

§25. Relative to the further use of DE in Petronius, as in other plebeian writers, one cannot go far in his inquiry without observing the tendency to employ DE where he would ordinarily look for a Partitive Genitive in classic language. In fact, both Röensch and Diez have shown that this usage became more and more common during the declining[1] periods of the language, finally appearing in its well known form in French, as well as in the other languages of the Romance group. In Petronius I find these instances: §§44,18: "Nomina omnia reddere, tanquam unus de nobis"; 58,24: "Qui de[2] nobis longe venio, late venio?"; 58,25: "Qui de nobis currit....; qui de nobis crescit", etc.; 66,9: "De scriblita quidem non minimum[3] edi"; 26,22: "Ut.... sciat, quantum de vita perdiderit"; 66,14: "De quo cum imprudens Scintilla gustasset"; 75,26: "Quia non sum de gloriosis"; 115,26: "De tam magna nave ne tabulam.... habes"; 115,42: "Ne quid de nobis relinquat sepultura".

In connection with the foregoing facts of Petronian usage, it is interesting to bear in mind that in the best writers of the classical period this latter use of DE in place of the Partitive Genitive occurs mainly either to avoid ambiguity where genitives would be multiplied, or for greater precision[4]. In the first instance cf. Cic. Cat. 2,1,12: "Ut aliquem partem de istius impudentia reticere possim"; in the second, cf. Cic. Tusc. 4,7,16: "Si quae sunt de eodem genere"; also Id. Phil. 2,27,65: "Persona de mimo"; and, in fact, in a considerable number of other passages in Cicero do we find this usage; e. g. Att. 8,12: "Hominem certum misi de[5] comitibus meis"; and Mil. 24,65: "Gladio percussus ab uno de[5] illis", etc.

---

1 See also many examples cited by Bonnet, pp. 610-613 [La Latinité de Grégoire de Tours]; and H. Goelzer [La Latinité de Saint Jérôme], p. 342.

2 I have followed Bücheler's emendation, which seems to be reasonable; first, in view of the MS reading, which is hardly translatable: QUIDEM VONIS; and secondly, in view of the line following, where DE is thus used, evidently in a continuation of the preceding thought.

3 Cf. also, §66,10: "De melle me usque tetigi"; and §75,23: "Labra de lucerna unguebam."

4 Vid. Freund, Lex. p. 513.

5 Cf. Also this use of DE in late Latin; e. g. Luc. 16,17: "Quam de lege (= τοῦ νόμου) unum apicem cadere." Gall. Rehd. Amiat. Vulg.; also "Gratuitum de deo (= τοῦ θεοῦ) munus", Cyprian ad Donat. 13; etc.

§26. Let us next turn to the most common signification of DE in extant[1] Latin, comparable in this sense with the Greek περί, and consider its use in Petronius. At the outset, I may say that I have found this usage proportionately less frequent than several of the earlier ones, this being due, doubtless, to an extended use in Plebeian Latin of this preposition in other senses, rather than to a loss in this sense. The instances follow:

§§13,6: "....rediisse ad nos thesaurum de quo querebar,'; 17,18: "Sed de remedio non tam valde laboro"; 18,11: "Si non admissetis de hac medicina"; 35,14: "De Laserpiciario mimo canticum extorsit"; 43,6: "De re tamen ego verum dicam"; 46,19: "Volo illum....aliquid de[2] jure gustare"; 48,20: "Numquid duodecim aerumnas Herculis tenes, aut de Ulixe fabulam?" 62,29: "Viderint alii quid de hoc exopinissent"; 85,5: "Quotiescumque.. de usu formosorum mentio facta est"; 141,16: "De stomachi tui recusatione non habeo quod timeam".

§27. Passing now to another fact of Petronian usage, I have found some half-dozen or more cases in which DE is used to indicate the place from which motion proceeds, or from which something is brought or has its origin, as in Plaut. Asin., 2,2,10: "De tergo plagas dare", etc.; and in a large number of passages from Cicero[3] and other writers of the classical period:

§§30,6: "Lucerna bilychnis de camera pendebat"; 38,13: "De nihilo crevit"; 60,5: "...Quid novi de caelo nuntiaretur"; 60,6: "Circulus ingens de cupa....demittitur"; 67,21: "Quae de cervice sua capsellam detraxit"; 70,27: "Paene de lectis dejecti sumus"; 74,8: "De vicinia gallus allatus est".

The three remaining instances of this usage occur in the

---

1 E. g. Cic Lael. 1,1: "Multa narrare de Laelio"; Id. Fam. 3,10,15: "Dubitare de re"; etc , etc.

2 The use of DE in this passage may, perhaps equally well, fall into the classification described in the 1 receding paragraph; i.e. the use of DE in place of the more common Partitive Genitive.

3 E. g. "Haec agebantur in conventu, palam, de sella ac de loco superiore". Cic. Verr., 2,4,40; cf also Id. Ib. 2,2,38; et Ib. 2,5,7: "Quem .... de tribunali citari jussit," etc.

4 Cf. Mt. 3,9: "De (= ἐκ) lapidibus istis suscitare"; Gall. Amiat.Vulg. 19,12: "De (= ἐκ) utero matris nati sunt sic", etc. Cf. also Aug. Civ. XX, 4: "Testimonia prius elige ida sunt de libris instrumenti novi, postea de veteris". Other examples are to be found in Spartian, Get. 5; Capitol. Macrin. 15; Lampr. Heliog. 19 23,24; Gallieu. 16; Vopisc. Aurel. 35,49; Treb. Poll. Claud. 14. See Rönsch, pp. 395, 396.

poetic fragments, viz.: (1) "Idaco quales fudit de vertice flores terra parens...," §127,27; (2) "Haec ubi personuit, de caelo Delphicus ales omina laeta dedit," etc., §122,177; (3) "Hinc molli stillae lacus et de caudice lento vimineae lances", etc., §135,26.

§28. Before concluding this brief sketch of DE, as it occurs in our author, mention should be made of the few remaining cases. In §45,31 occur the words, "Occidit de¹ lucerna equites," where the force of the preposition is virtually the same as in Cic. Att., 4,3,4: "In comitium Milo de nocte venit"; et Id. Mur., 9,22: "Vigilas tu de² nocte"; and Caes. B. G. VII, 45: "Caesar mittit complures equitum turmas eo de media nocte", etc.

§29. Another use of DE, though rare in Petronius, appears in §75,9 and in §77,2, the function of the preposition in these instances obviously being to indicate the property from which the cost of some object is taken: "Archisellium de suo paravit et duas trullas" (75,9), and "Tu dominam tuam de rebus illis fecisti" (77,2). Examples of this usage I have found to be fairly common in Cicero, Livy and Suetonius³, and, I doubt not, in other authors as well. Cicero, Ad. Quint. Fratr., 1,3,7 says: "Cum de visceribus tuis satisfacturus sis quibus debes"; and in Att., 16,16, as in A. 5, the same writer uses "de suo" exactly as it appears in the first example from Petronius which I have cited above.

§30. Finally, in §14,22, may be found the only parallel, I think, to the use of DE in Cic. Cael. 29: "De suorum propinquorum sententia atque auctoritate fecisse dicatur"; et Id. Verr., 2,5,21: "De consilii sententia Mamertinis se frumentum non imperare pronunciat", etc.⁴ Petronius

---

1 My first impression led me to explain this use of DE as I have here classified it. A better understanding of the passage, however, has since convinced me that the preposition points, figuratively, to the *origin* of the EQUITES; i.e. the latter were "mere ghosts" of horsemen.

2 Cf. also Cic. ad Quint. Fratr., 2,1 (end): "Navigare de mense Decembri"; and Suetonius, Vesp. §21: "De nocte evigilabat"; etc.

3 e. g. Liv. VI, 15,10; Suet. Caes. §19; etc.

4 Cf. also Cic. Att. 4,2,4: "Vix de mea voluntate concessum est"; and Virg. Aen., XI, 14,2: "De more vetusto"; and Ovid, Met., 7,105; etc.

says: "Nostram scilicet de more ridebant invidiam", or, as the Greek might say: κατὰ τὸν τρόπον, or some similar expression.

§31. It seems appropriate at this point to state that I have found three facts of Ciceronian usage in regard to DE which are not, to my knowledge, exemplified in Petronius. For example, in Cic. Att., 12,3, we read: "Velim scire hodierne statim de auctione aut quo die venias", where the preposition clearly has its rare signification of "directly¹ after." Then again in Cic. Att. 7,7,3, and frequently elsewhere, DE is used to indicate the producing cause or reason; viz.: "Nam id nisi gravi de causa fecisset", etc. The other form of usage is DE with adjectives to form adverbial expressions².

§32. The tendency in late and vulgar Latin to employ both DE and CUM with the Accusative case, does not appear in Petronius. A very interesting collection of examples of this form of usage has been made by Rönsch,³ who points out, among others, the following instances: "De Johannem testimonium dicit", Cod. Rehd. Capit. Luc. VI; also Sulp. Sev. Ep. III, 4: "de obitum" (Cod. Veron.); and "de modum", Gromat. Vett. p. 6,16; and "cum officiales", Gest. purgat. Felic. p. 84, u. 87 (ap. Baluz. II); and "Sic te egisse cum filium tuum", Gest. purgat. Caecilian. ib. p. 98; etc.

§33. Another form of expression, found occasionally in classic⁴ poetry, but more especially in the African writers and in ecclesiastical Latin, namely, the use of DE instead of the simple Instrumental Ablative, I have not discovered in this author. Cf. Apul. Met. 53: "De latronis huius sanguine

---

1 There are three interesting examples of this usage in Lucr., VI, 29c: "Quo de concussu"; I, 384: "De concursu"; et Id., V, 651: "De longo cursu sol......". Liv. 5,48, has: "Diem de die", etc. Cf. also Vulg. Psa., 60,8, and other passages in ecclesiastical Latin. In reference to the use of DE in the sense of "after," Munro (ad Lucr., Vol. II, p. 63) has observed that Faber quotes Plaut., Most. 697: "Non bonust somnus de prandio"; and Verg. Aen., II, 662: "Jamque aderit multo Priami de sanguine Pyrrhus."

2 This usage is frequent both in Caesar and in Cicero; e. g. "De improviso" occurs in Caes. B.G., 2,3; 5,22; 5,39; et saep.; and in Cic. Rosc. Am., 52,131, et saep. Cf. also "De transverso", Cic. Att., 15,4 (end); etc., etc.

3 pp. 409-410.

4 e. g. Terence, Adel., I, 2,33: "Ne me obtundas de hac re saepius".

legibus vestris....litate"; Id. 189: "Verberoni sua placuit
salus de mea morte"; cf. also Hildebrand ad Apul. Met.[1];
also "De tessella sua recludis", Apic. 4,5; "Eas de hoc jure
perfundis....de sabano calido involves gruem" (Cod.Vatic.)
Id. 6,2; "De fustibus caesus", Amm. Marc. 29,3; and "Quid
potestas Martia de habitu prudentiae valeat", Id. 31,5; and
other examples which might be cited.

PART IV—IN.

§34. We have now considered, more or less fully, some
of the central facts of Petronian usage in the employment
of three leading prepositions, and in doing this we have
noted the essential points of coincidence, or of divergence,
between this usage and that of the classical or Ciceronian
period. Let us turn, then, to an examination of the preposition IN.

In the first place, one may be somewhat surprised, upon
investigation, to find that there are more than five hundred[1]
instances of this word in a narrative of scarcely four
thousand[2] lines. Perhaps this is not an abnormal propor-
tion; yet it exceeds that of AD by nearly 100%! Furthermore, I have observed that about three fourths of the
various forms of usage in which the preposition IN plays a
part in classic Latin are represented, more or less distinctly,
in the writings of Petronius. These, as well as those forms
which are not so represented, I shall try to indicate in the
course of this discussion, at the same time noting, as far as
possible, any instances of plebeian usage.

§35. I pass, then, to the details of the subject-matter.
In Petronius, as in Latin literature generally, the two by
far most common functions of the preposition IN are seen

---

[1] pp. 164 and 229.

[2] These figures include the poetic passages. The latter, however, are not included
in the detailed examination of the syntax. To speak exactly, there are in all 524
instances of this preposition in Petronius, 41 of which occur in poetry.

(1) in a literal sense (cf. Eng. "within"), as in Cic. Tusc. I,9,19: "Alii in corde, alii in cerebro dixerunt animi esse sedem et locum", etc.; and (2) with verbs of motion. The passages included in the former of these classes are the following: §§1,8; 2,1; 3,1; 3,2; 3,7; 4,12 (bis); 6,2 (bis); 7,10; 7,12; 9,18; 12,1[1]; 12,5; 12,12; 17,18; 17,20; 19,5, 21,14[2]; 21,19; 24,7; 24,16; 25,17[3]; 26,21; 27,8; 28,4[4]; 28,8; 28,17; 28,18; 29,10; 29,14; 29,15 (bis); 29,17; 29,19; 30,1; 30,19; 30,21; 31,19[5](bis); 33,9; 34,10; 35,3; 35,8; 35,9; 35,12; 36,4; 36,7; 37,14; 37,15; 38,29; 39,5; 39,19 (bis); 39,10[6]; 39,29; 39,31; 40,8; 43,18; 43,23; 44,13 (bis); 44,15; 45,11; 47,14[7]; 47;18; 47,23; 48,4; 48,21; 50,3; 52,6; 31,20; 53,8; 53,16; 53,20; 53,23; 56,13; 57,10; 57,17; 57,25; 57,32; 58,27; 61,3; 61,11; 62,8; 62,25; 64,23; 66,2; 66,4; 66,11; 66,19; 66,21; 70,20; 71,4; 71,17[9]; 71,27[9]; 71,34; 72,12; 73,4; 73,5; 73,21[10]; 74,6; 74,31; 76,1; 76,14; 77,11; 80,25; 81,2; 81,10; 81,16; 83,12 (bis); 90,1; 91,9; 91,15; 94,3; 94,35; 97,1[11]; 97,4, 98,23; 99,4[12]; 99,10; 100,4; 102,14; 104,4; 104,5; 105,2; 105,5; 106,8; 106,17; 108,15; 109,15; 111,6; 111,13[13]; 111,17; 115,16; 116,11; 116,14[14]; 116,15; 116,22[15]; 117,25; 125,4; 129,3; 129,21 (bis); 132,31; 132,44; 135,11; 140,7; 140,9; 141,5.

---

1 "In quo (sc. foro) notavimus frequentiam", etc.

2 "In qua (sc. cella) tres lecti strati sunt", etc.

3 "In secreto"; cf. §97,1 and §129,3; cf. also Livy, XXVI, 19,5; and Curt. 10,4,29.

4 "In conspectu", as in §111,4; cf. Cic. Fam. 1,7,5. The latter writer, however (Verr. 2,5,66, §170: "In conspectu legum libertatisque moriatur"), uses this expression of inanimate as well as of animate objects. Petronius employs it in reference to animate objects only. A. O.

5 ".....olivas in altera parte albas, in altera nigras"; cf. §27,8: "In diversa parte circuli stabant."

6 "In quo (sc. caelo) duodecim dii habitant."

7 "Anathymiasis ....in toto corpore fluctum facit."

8 "Ut sint in fronte (sc. statuae meae) pedes centum", etc.

9 "In publico"; cf. §100,4; see also remarks on pp. 29–30 (§56, fin.) of this paper.

10 See note on "Iu conspectu" (Note 4 above). The same words occur here.

11 See note on §25,17 (Note 3, above).

12 ".....neque enim in amantium esse potestate furiosam aemulationem."

13 "Una igitur in tota civitate fabula erat."

14 ".....quoscunque homines in hac urbe videritis", etc.

15 "In quibus (sc. campis) nihil aliud est nisi cadavera, quae lacerantur", etc

§36. In the great majority of these instances which I have tabulated, the language of Petronius is fully in accord with the laws of Ciceronian usage. There are, however, some cases in which differences exist, and it is to these that I now wish to call attention. In §19,5 we read: "Vetui.... in hoc deversorio quemquam mortalium admitti", where the Accusative case with AD or IN after "admittere" would almost instinctively be looked for. Here, as in other instances which I shall have occasion to point out later, a glimpse may be had of the gradual confusion between the cases, which arose in the popular speech, and which is at times marked by an indifferent use of IN with the Accusative or Ablative.

An interesting parallel to the passage just cited occurs in §26,25, the MS. reading of which is: "Gitona....jubemus IN BALNEO[1] SEQUI", emended unnecessarily, it seems to me, by Bücheler[2], who reads "IN BALNEA SEQUI", a combination doubtless more euphonious and grammatically correct, on the basis of the highest literary standard. But, as Ludwig[3] has rightly shown, certain deviations in syntax from that standard not only occur in the *Sermo Plebeius*, but in many instances may be more or less clearly defined.

§37. A second use of IN, equally frequent in Petronius, is the ordinary classic construction with the Accusative case after verbs of motion, viz:

§§1,7 (bis); 4,5; 6,3; 7,4; 7,8; 7,9; 8,6; 9,2; 9,8; 11,1; 12,1 (1); 15,16; 15,18; 16,11; 18,9[4]; 21,14 (1); 21,18[5]; 22,1; 24,15; 25,6; 26,5; 27,11; 29,11; 31,8; 33,2; 33,18;

---

1 It is interesting to compare with this passage the MS. reading of §73,16: "In solo descendimus," which we again find emended by Bücheler (p. 49) to read "In solium", etc. Scheffer has "In solio", etc., which I believe to be nearer the correct reading. Cf. Friedländer, p. 184. Note also the phrases "In praesidio dare," Hygin. f. 52; "In concilio adducere", f. 92; etc.

2 "Petronii Satirae (iii Ed.), p. 19 (Berlin, 1895); cf. Friedländer, p. 72 (Leipsig, 1891).

3 "De Petronii Sermone Plebeio," p. 36 (Marburg, 1869).

4 "In risum mota (sc. mulier); cf. §10,5: "In risum diffusi"; also cf. §18,18: "In tantum repente risum effusa est"; and §49,18: "Relaxato in hilaritatem vultu."

5 "Cum laberemur in somnum"; i.e. Figurative motion. Cf. the same expression in §22,1 and in §87,15; also "In soporem labentis," §100,19; "In somnum decidi," §87,20.

34,11[1]; 37,7; 37,17; 38,5[2]; 41,8; 41,23; 41,25; 42,9; 42,17;
44,33; 47,14 (1); 47,19; 47,32; 48,1; 50,12; 51,4; 53,4;
53,6; 57,13[3]; 57,29; 58,14[4]; 58,29; 62,12; 62,24; 63,16;
65,8; 65,15; 67,3; 69,12; 70,22; 71,24; 72,6; 72,14; 72,16;
72,18; 73,18; 74,4; 74,10; 74,30; 74,37; 75,6; 76,22; 78,2;
78,12; 79,23; 80,21; 82,2[5]; 83,1; 83,15; 83,16; 85,1; 85,9;
85,11; 86,19; 87,3; 87,15[6]; 87,20[6]; 88,20; 91,10; 91,26; 92,5;
92,8; 95,6; 96,10; 99,4 (1); 100,19[6]; 101,10; 101,24; 102,3;
102,20; 102,24; 102,53; 103,16; 105,3; 105,36; 107,3;
107,21; 107,30; 108,38; 109,25; 110,2; 111,5; 111,22;
111,26; 112,15; 112,29; 113,5; 113,25; 114,14; 115,8;
115,31; 116,2; 125,9; 126,21; 126,26; 128,13; 129,4;
131,2; 131,12; 131,31; 134,6; 134,15; 135,4; 135,17;
136,2; 136,10; 136,27; 137,5; 137,34 (bis); 138,22; 140,12;
140,43; 140,45.

§38. As might naturally be expected in a survey of this
kind, I have drawn a distinction between the use of IN in
what may be called its literal" sense and its use as indicating the analogous relation of the place or position of two or
more objects; a very frequent form of usage, of course, in
classical as well as in plebeian Latin. Of the many
examples from Cicero, the following will serve as a model,
by way of comparison: "Ipse coronam habebat unam in
capite, alteram in collo," Cic. Verr., 2,5,11, §27; "...sedere
in equo," Ib., 2,5,10. From Petronius I have collated in
all 55 instances of this usage, indicating in footnotes or

---

1 An odd usage of IN: "Vinumque dedere in manus." Cf. §57,13. N.B.—Anent the
expression "dare in manus," it is interesting to note that in Cicero we find "sumere in
manus," and in Livy "tradere" used in the same way; but not "dare," I believe. Cf.
Liv., 5,27,3: "Falerios se in manus Romanis tradidisse"; cf. also "Alicui rem iu manum
tradere," Liv., 1,54,10; 26,12,11. See Ballas, Die Phraseologie des Livius, p. 23.

2 After he had bought rams from Tarentum, the narrative says, Trimalchio "testi-
culavit in gregem," which appears to be a unique expression. Cf. Fest., p. 366, Müll.:
"Testiculari est jumentis maribus feminas vel mares feminis admovere, licet alii dicant
testilari." In other words, Trimalchio wished to improve the breed of his domestic
livestock.

3 "Me dedi in servitutem"; cf. §34,11 and Note.

4 "In rutae folium conjecero." The same expression occurs in §37,17; q.v.

5 "In publicum prosilio," as in §95,6: "Fugere in publicum voluistis."

6 See note on §21,18.

7 See Part IV (p. 18) of this discussion.

otherwise any passages which seem to call for special comment:

§§1,10; 3,13; 9,1; 20,4; 22,7; 26,15; 28,14; 28,16; 29,4; 30,3; 30,5; 30,8; 32,1; 32,6; 34,16; 38,12; 40,4; 47,11; 57,22 (bis); 59,8; 59,18; 62,26; 63,5; 67,9 (bis); 67,33; 70,11; 70,17; 71,26; 74,39; 77,18; 79,13; 85,5; 85,12; 86,15; 88,11; 97,7; 99,15; 107,14; 111,13 (1); 113,9; 126,22; 127,34; 128,25; 133,6; 134,2; 134,3; 135,6; 136,33; 137,10; 137,36; 140,19 and 20; 141,28.

§39. Continuing our survey of IN with the Ablative case in Petronius we find but a half-dozen instances of its use as in Cic. Leg., 2,11,26, et Id. Fam., 13,78,2, where the preposition clearly has a partitive or inclusive signification, viz.: (1) "Thales qui sapientissimus in septem fuit," or (2) "Peto ut eum complectare, diligas, in tuis habeas," etc. Petronius has the passages following:

§§26,9: "...in primis[1] Quartilla per rimam...applicuerat oculum"; 57,35: "Quid nunc stupes tanquam hircus in ervilia"; 71,38: "Cum posset in onmibus decuriis Romae esse..."; 82,9: "In exercitu vestro phaecasiati milites ambulant"; 126,16: "Et in extrema plebe quaerit quod diligat".

§40. The indication of time duration by IN and the Ablative is another interesting form of usage[2], seven examples of which I have found in Petronius:

§§3,5: "Nimirum in his[3] exercitationibus doctores peccant"; 4,13: "Quod....turpius est, in senectute confiteri non vult"; 31,10: "In hoc[3] tam molesto tacebant officio"; 44,24: "Plus in die nummorum accipit quam alter"; 45,7: "Habituri sumus munus excellente in triduo die festa"; 62,15: "Gladium tamen strinxi, et in tota via umbras cecidi"; 141,25: "Nec quicquam in hac epulatione captabant,...."

§41. Furthermore, I have observed in Petronius some twenty odd instances in which IN is used in reference to a

---

1 Cf. the frequent use of the adverbial "IMPRIMIS" in classic Latin; e.g. Nepos, Att., 13,1; also in Cic., Sall., etc. I have failed to find "IMPRIMIS" in Petronius.

2 Cf. Sall., Cat 48,5: "In tali tempore"; also Cic. Brut., 43 (fin.): "In qua aetate, ..."; also Id Verr., 2,3,91: "Nihil in vita se simile fecisse," etc.

3 i.e. During the time of performance.

certain condition or situation in which some person or thing
is placed; cf. Caes., Bell. Civ. III, 31: "Summa in solici-
tudine ac timore Parthici belli," etc.; and Cic., Cat., 2,8,18:
".... qui magno in aere alieno majores etiam possessiones
habent," etc. It may be added that this use of IN is frequent throughout the whole range of classic prose, both
ante- and post-Augustan[1]. The examples from Petronius[2]
follow:

§§43,6; 55,1; 59,4; 61,20; 63,8[3]; 66,13; 83,11; 98,8; 98,25;
98,26; 101,26; 108,1; 111,27; 115,4; 116,22 (1); 129,8;
139,15; 141,25 (1).

§42. Of the use of IN with the Accusative case to denote
the simple limit of motion, I have already spoken. Let us
now turn to its employment in other relations, noting first
the following instances which I have grouped together, and
in which the function of the preposition may be conceived as
indicating an "aiming at" or a "striving towards" something;
cf. Cic. Off, 1,9,28: "Id quod apud Platonem est in phil-
osophos dictum...," etc., etc. Petronius, for the most part,
follows classic usage in this mode of expression:

§§46,11[4]; 48,24; 50,13[5]; 39,10[5](2); 58,3; 77,3; 90,1;
94,33; 95,18; 96,11; 99,19; 105,35; 108,7[5]; 108,13; 109,27;
110,7; 110,16; 114,38[5]; 130,5[6]; 132,49; 136,13; 140,31[7];
141,7[5].

§43. A familiar passage from Caes., Bell. Gall.[8] leads
me, at this point, to speak of the use of IN as an indication

---

1 Cf. Georges' Lexikon der Lateinischen Wortformen, p. 343; also Freund,
Lex. s. IN.

2 Exclusive of this usage in the poetic passages; e.g. §14,10 and §55,28.

3 "Cum.....nos in tristimonio essemus"; elsewhere "tristimonia" appears to be used.

4 "In aves morbosus," i.e. passionately fond of birds. A curious expression. Cf.
"In argento studiosus," §52,1. See p. 31 of this paper. The words are here put into
the mouth of the orator, Agamemnon, by the rag-dealer, Echion.

5 In the passages marked 5, the preposition is used to denote rather the result of
an act or effort, or to express some change of one object INTO another.

6 "In haec facinora quaere supplicium," etc.

7 "Qui me restituerunt in integrum". Perhaps in this instance the preposition
with its following adjective may be taken in an adverbial sense; cf. especially th s
usage in "Silver" Latin; e.g. Tac. G. 5: "In universum" (i.e. "in general"); and Plin.,
16,40,79, §217: "In plenum" (i.e. "fully"), etc. See p. 24 of this survey.

8 "Belgae spectant in septentriones et orientem solem"; cf. also Tac. 1c:
"In orientem Germaniae, in occidentem Hispaniae obtenditur, Gallis in meridiem
inspicitur."

of mere direction "towards," of which Petronius has the following six cases:

§§9,11: "Intentavi in oculos Ascylti manus," etc.; 34,23: "Ut articuli ejus....in omnem partem flecterentur"; 70,14: "Intentavimus oculos in proeliantes"; 110,21: "Conversis igitur omnium in se vultibus," etc.; 115,21: "Cum inviolatum os fluctus convertit in terram"; 140,39: "Quod nunquam in tabernam conspexerat".

§44. Again, there are some six or seven passages which may be compared with Cic., Fam. 7,3: "In mentem venire"; or with Liv., 27,9: "In animum inducere"; i.e. cases in which something is thought of as entering the mind or feelings:

§§10,7: "Rursus in memoriam revocatus," etc.; 41,2: "In multas cogitationes deductus sum"; 53,11: "Ideo in rationem nondum venerunt"; 53,13: "In rationes meas inferri vetuo"; 81,4: "Redeunte in animum solitudine"; 113,6: "Non dubie redierat in animum Hedyle".

§45. I have found a single instance in Petronius in which IN is used exactly as in Horace, Ep. I, 18[1]; cf. also Cic., Fam. 5,15,1: "Nisi id verbum in omne tempus perdidissem". The passage to which I refer is §73,24: "Itaque tengomenas faciamus et usque in lucem cenemus," where the preposition clearly points to time-duration.

§46. The expression "In domusionem tamen literas didici" occurs in §48,10, where the meaning of the prepositional phrase appears to be precisely the same as in §46,19. In the latter passage, however, AD is used ("Ad domusionem aliquid de jure gustare"). This employment of IN by Petronius, in reference to some object in view, with the suggestion of motive[2], finds its only parallel in this author in §69,8: "Et ideo me in vilicationem relegavit," where the boasting Trimalchio speaks of his former master's having commissioned him to be bailiff, etc.

§47. There are some three or four instances where IN

---

[1] "Dormiet in lucem."

[2] Cf. Cic., Fam. 13,1,16; also Virg. Aen. II, 347: "Quos ardere in proelia vidi"; and Livy, XXI, 45,4: "Certa praemia quorum in spem pugnarent"; etc.

is used to form adverbial expressions, a type of usage not uncommon in classic Latin, and especially among writers of the so-called Silver[1] period:

§§18,12: "Jam parata in crastinum[2] erat turba"; 33,10: "Gallina lignea patentibus in orbem[3] alis"; 50,15: "Sic Corinthia nata sunt, ex omnibus in unum"; 86,14: "Deinde in unum omnia vota conjunxi".

§48. In conclusion, mention should be made of certain uses of IN which do not appear in Petronius, but which are more or less frequent in Cicero and other classic writers. First, "In tempore," i.e. "at the right or proper time," as in Livy, 33,5[4]: "Ni pedites equitesque in tempore subvenissent"; secondly, "In praesentia," and "In praesenti," i.e. "now," "at present," "under these circumstances," etc., as in Cic. Tusc., 1,8,14: "Sic enim mihi in praesentia occurrit"; and Livy, 21,37: "Id quod unum maxime in praesentia desiderabatur," etc.; thirdly, the use of IN with Gerunds and Fut. Pass. Participles, to indicate duration of time; e. g. Cic. Off., 1,3,9: "Fit ut distrahatur in deliberando animus," etc.; fourthly, the use of IN with the Ablative of adjectives in conjunction with the verbs "esse" and "habere" to express quality; e. g. Cic. Fam., 15,16,3: "In integro esse"; also Livy, 39,37,14: "I ı aequo esse"; et Id., 3,8,9: "Cum exitus hand in facili (=faciles) essent," etc. It is noticeable that this form of usage is confined mostly to adjectives of the first and second declensions.

§49. Lastly, the use of IN in the phrase "In rem esse," (i. e. "to be useful," "to avail," etc.), which is found in Sallust[5], Livy and Virgil, and perhaps in other classic writers, does not appear in Petronius. Nor do we find in this author, as far as I have observed, any instances of the

---

1 e. g. Tac. Germ., 5: "In universum" (=in general); and Plin., 16,40,79, §217: "In plenum" (=fully), etc.

2 The expression "In crastinum" occurs at least twice in Plautus, viz.: Pseud. 5,2,55 ("In crastinum vos vocabo"), and Cas., 3,5,60.

3 This use of "In orbem" I have found also in §102,49: "Numquid et crura in orbem pandere?"

4 I have also found examples of this use in Terence and in Tacitus; cf. also Lucretius, Bk. I, 1037. Cicero, however, employs simply "tempore," without the preposition.

5 e. g. "In rem fore credens universos adpellare," etc., Sall. Cat., 20,1.

late use of IN with the Ablative in place of[1] the simple Ablative of Instrument; e. g. "Virgam in qua percussisti flumen," Aug. Locut. 89 d. Exod.; "Bibere in ossibus capitum," Flor. III, 4,2; "Statuam in aere auratam posuere," Inser. Vet. Hispan. It is perhaps hardly necessary to add that Petronius never employs the Genitive or the Dative case after any of the prepositions which we are here considering, although a few examples of this usage are seen in late vulgar Latin. Rönsch[2] calls attention to an instance of CUM with the Genitive, as well as to one passage in which IN is similarly used, or else is followed by the Dative, the noun being a word of the first declension.

§50. It remains to speak of three odd instances in which the preposition IN is followed by the Accusative[3], where the Ablative would ordinarily be expected. It will be noticed that in two of these instances the verb "esse" is found:

§§15,8: "Neque enim res tantum....in controversiam esse"; 42,4: "Fui enim hodie in funus"; 58,12: "Videbo te in publicum".

This form of usage, although usually regarded as plebeian, finds expression similarly in Cicero[4], Livy and Quintilian. It is, however, especially noticeable in the *Sermo Plebeius*, as Muncker and others[5] have shown. Plautus, Amphitr. I, 1,25, has "In mentem esse," and a number of other examples might be cited. Cf. Gessner. Thesaur. Rustic.: "In fornacem coquere," Cat. r. r. 39.2; "In curiam fuerunt," Grut. 214; "Mansi in solitudinem," Mon. miss. p. 47; "In fines ponere," "In medium esse," Faust. et Valer. Grom., p. 308.

§51. This tendency in plebeian and rustic speech toward the use of prepositions with cases other than those

---

[1] Rönsch, pp. 396-397, has collected many examples of this usage in *late* writers; q.v.

[2] Id. p. 412.

[3] Madvig, Gram., §230, Obs. 2, regards the Accusative after "esse," "habere," etc., as probably originating in an error of pronunciation; a theory which may reasonably be doubted.

[4] e. g. Verr. 2,5,38 "Quod, qui illam partem urbis tenereut, in eorum potestatem portum futurum intellegebant."

[5] Cf. Rönsch, pp. 406, 407, and pp. 410-412; cf. also Studer, —M. Rh. II, p. 79.

regularly employed in classic prose and poetry, as I have
intimated, finds few examples in Petronius, who in this
respect usually follows the laws of standard latinity. Viola-
tion of these laws, however, is observed not only in the passages which I have cited on pp. 28–29, but also in §39,26:
"Quibus prae mală suă cornua nascuntur"; and in §46,4:
"Scimus te prae literas fatuum esse." Both von Guericke
and Ludwig, and especially Rönsch¹, have collected a large
number of examples from late writers as well as from
Pompeian inscriptions.

§52. Turning again to the three instances of IN referred
to in the preceding section, it may be worth while for us to
note that the words "Neque enim res tantum, quae vide-
rentur, in controversiam esse," are put into the mouth of the
hero of the story, Encolpius, the use of the preposition here
being comparable with that in the remark made at Trimalchio's banquet by the guest Seleucus, when he says, in
describing the death of his friend Chrysanthus, "Fui enim
hodie in funus." (Cf. the vulgar English, "I was TO a funeral
to-day.") What the speaker means, of course, is, as von
Guericke² has suggested: "Contuli me in funus, et adfui."
In the same way, in §58,12, the opponent of Ascyltus, in a
little tilt which has occurred, says to the jocose but insup-
pressible boy Giton, "Videbo te in publicum," or as one
might say in English, under similar circumstances, "I'll see
you outside," the meaning clearly being, as von Guericke
again aptly points out, "Curabo, ut venias in publicum et in
publico te videbo." Similarly Plautus, Men. 865, has "Astiti
in currum"; cf. also "Jacēre in locum" (Corp. Inscr. Lat. II,
3354); "Manere in amicitiam" (Corp. Inscr. Lat. I, 200);
"Quiescit in pacem" (Corp. Inscr. Christ. 101, a.348), and
other examples cited by Plew and Rönsch.³

---

1 Cf. von Guer., pp. 56-58; Ludwig, p. 36; Rönsch, pp. 406-412. Cf. also Bonuet,
"La Latinité de Grégoire de Tours," pp. 616-620.

2 De Ling. Vulg., p. 58.

3 See Plew, "De Diversitate Auctorum Historiae Augustae," p. 41; Rönsch, pp.
410 sqq.

§53. Von Guericke[1], in his valuable little work on Petronian vulgarisms, to which I have already referred, alludes to the passage, "In cenam fieri" (§47,24), as an instance in which IN is equal to AD, and states that this confusion of prepositions seems to have arisen through carelessness of thought on the part of the uneducated classes; and further, that the same cause explains the origin of those vulgar expressions such as "In deversorio admitti" (§19,7), "Voca cocum in medio" (§49,7), and "In balneo sequi" (§26,25). Moreover, he declares that this form of usage appears, in fact, in the "*Oratio Urbana*," but that it is, perhaps, an imitation of the "*Sermo Rusticus*". I must concur with von Guericke in being unable to find the passage cited by Ludwig[2] as §77, "In balneo descendere"; the nearest to which I have found to be in §73,16, which reads, according to Bücheler, "In solium descendimus," the MS. reading, however, being "In solo descendimus". But to this passage I have referred elsewhere[3].

§54. The use of IN with the Ablative in the sense of the Greek εἰς appears not only in a considerable number of instances both in vulgar and ecclesiastical Latin, but is also found very rarely in Cicero, Nepos, and Ovid, and perhaps in other classical representatives as well. Cf. Cic., Nat. Deor. I, "Ne in cogitatione quidem cadit"; also Id. Som. Scip. 3, "Pietas in[4] (=AD) parentibus et in patria". Also Nepos, Phoc. 4: "In hoc tantum fuit odium multitudinis"; and Ovid, Trist. V, 2,36: "Saepe suo victor lenis in hoste fuit"; also Id. Metam. IV, 546; and Amor. I, 7,34. Among late writers many examples have been noted by Rönsch[5], a few of which I here quote for convenience of comparison: Mt. 12,9, "Venit in synagoga"; Id. 13,2, "In (=εἰς) navi ascendens"; Id. 13,7, "Ceciderunt in spinis"; Id. 13,47,

1 De Ling. Vulg. Reliq., p. 58.

2 p. 36.

3 See p. 20 of this paper, especially *Note 1*.

4 Cf. Orell. Inscr. 159: "Pius in suis."

5 pp. 406 407.

"Missae in mari"; Id. 24,16, "Fugiat in montibus"; Id. 26,52, "Converte gladium tuum in loco suo"; Lucif. Athan. II, p. 135; I Sam. 26,6, "Quis introibit mecum in (=εἰς) castris," etc., Lucif. Athan. 1,30. Cf. also "Et insufflavit in oculis," Reg.Germ. 4; "Mitto vos tamquam oves in medio¹ luporem," Tert. Scorp. 9; "Tradidit eos in manibus diripientium," Scorp. 3; and "In solitudine translatus," Bapt. 20; and further, "In tabulis referre,". Flor. 1,6; "In adjutorio vocavit," Hygin. Fab. 190; and "Adhibitis in consilio suo consulibus," Spartian. Hadr. 22; etc.

§55. Another interesting and uncommon use of IN is found in Petronius, §79,1 : "Neque fax ulla in praesidio erat, quae iter aperiret errantibus," etc. Here the prepositional phrase closely resembles in meaning the use of the simple Dative of the Double Dative construction. Cf. Terence, Phorm. 2,1: "In lucro esse alicui," and the modern French, "Dieu vous soit en aide," etc.² Moreover, in §21,1 I have observed the only parallel in Petronius to the form of usage above mentioned, the passage being from a fragmentary, but very legible portion of the narrative: "Volebamus miseri exclamare, sed nec in auxilio erat quisquam," etc.

§56. A rare use of IN appears in §105,35 of the Petronian narrative, namely, with the verb "Durare": "Cuius tam crudeles manus in hoc supplicium durassent." This construction is not only rare, but is not found in ante-Augustan prose. Tacitus, Ann. I, 6, has one such case, viz.: "In nullius umquam suorum necem duravit," where the force of the preposition seems to be somewhat the same as in the examples cited on p. 24, §43, of this paper.

The phrase "in publico," to which I have referred else-where, occurs a few times in Petronius, and is, I think, vir-tually equivalent to the adverb "publice." On this point Ludwig³ has an interesting, although, it seems to me, hardly

---

1 Cf. Petronius, ?49,7.

2 Diez, Grammaire des Langues Romanes, p. 157 ff., calls attention to the Italian, "Che t' è in piacere?" and "Questo a me sarà in piacere" (Decam. 4,6).

3 p. 36.

convincing statement. In reference to Petronius, §71,27, "Nummos in publico....effundentem," he tabulates an irregularity, on the ground that in such an instance the Accusative would be expected. But I prefer to regard the expression as adverbial, as in Cic. Att., 8,9,2: "Epistulam in publico proponere," etc., and I see no cogent reason for any other classification. An exact parallel case is seen in Petronius, §100,4: "Quid aquis dici formosius potest? In publico tamen manant."

§57. Another interesting use of IN is with the verb "Demando'," instead of the more usual construction of this verb with the simple Dative, as in Livy, V., 27: "Simul plures pueri unius (sc. paedagogi) curae demandabantur"; et Id., 8,36: "Curam sauciorum militum legatis tribunisque (sc. demandare)". Petronius has one example of this verb with IN; §61,17: "Quicquid habui, in illius sinum demandavi," says Trimalchio's companion, Niceros, in his praise of the trustworthy qualities of a certain Melissa whom he admires. So in Suetonius, Calig. 9, occurs the expression "In proximam civitatem demandari," i. e. "to be sent for safety," etc. But even Suetonius usually prefers the simple Dative, as in his life of Julius Caesar, §83: "Testamentum virgini Vestali demandare."

The phrase "In oculis ferre," in the sense of "to love, esteem, or value," as in Cic., Phil., 6,4,11[2], is found once in Petronius, in the conversation between Trimalchio and the sevir Habinnas; §75,10: "Non est dignus quem in oculis feram?" or as Kelly[3] has well turned it in his English version of Petronius: "Does he (i. e. puer) not deserve that I should prize him as the apple of my eye?" So Terence Eun., 3,1[4], has a similar expression.

§58. Reference has already been made to the extended

---

1 This verb, in the sense of "commend," was apparently not in use before the time of Augustus. See the Lexicons, s.v.

2 "Oderat tum, cum......jam fert in oculis."

3 p. 276 (London, 1854).

4 "Rex te ergo in oculis," etc.

use in Petronius of prepositions in place of some of the
ordinary case-constructions in classic Latin. There is,
however, one passage to which I have not before alluded.
I refer to the words of Trimalchio in §52,1 : "In argento
plane studiosus sum," used to describe the latter's fondness
for silver. I have found no similar use of IN with "studiosus,"
although Varro, R. R., 1,17[1], has AD with this adjective.
But the simple Genitive is by far the most frequent form of
usage, and occurs in Cicero, Ovid, Horace, and Quintilian,
as well as in other writers. The Dative appears in some
few instances[2], though not in Petronius.

CONCLUSION.

We have now seen, in more or less minute detail, as a
result of the foregoing investigation, the main facts of
Petronian usage in reference to the features of syntax under
discussion. Among other points, we have observed, in general, (1) that Petronius exhibits a tendency, which gradually
found acceptance in later Latin, to employ prepositional
phrases in place of several of the more common case-
constructions of classic usage; e. g. the use of DE for the
so-called Partitive Genitive, and the occasional giving way
of the Dative of the Indirect Object to the construction
with AD, as well as certain other extended uses of prepositions, such as the participation of CUM in the function of the
Instrumental Ablative, etc. We have (2) also noticed,
though rarely, an apparent confusion between the use of the
Accusative and the Ablative, especially with AD or IN, and
in one or two passages with PRAE; and furthermore, (3)

---

1 "Studiosiores ad opus."

2 e. g. Suetonius, Jul. Caes., 46; also Sextus Aurelius Victor, Epitome 1; etc.

3 Cf. Plaut., Miles, 3,1,20.

we have been reminded, through the efforts of Rönsch, Wölfflin and other scholars, that the tendency of the Accusative to assume the functions of the other cases was a growing development in the language, amply illustrated in later writers.

In regard to the grammatical character of the language used by the different persons in the narrative of Petronius, it has been stated by Leonhard Schmitz[1] that "in this romance the hero Encolpius uses the language of a gentleman of the Augustan age, while most of the other speakers, especially Trimalchio, speak the language of the vulgar, uneducated people, full of all manner of irregularities." While to a great extent this assertion is undoubtedly true, yet in the matter of the use of some of the leading prepositions, at least, as I have tried to show, we occasionally find even in the words of the "gentlemanly" freedman Encolpius distinct traces of plebeian speech. On the other hand, the great majority of the utterances of the other persons in the story, including those of the upstart Trimalchio himself, are, from the point of view of the conventional standard in regard to prepositional usage, in excellent latinity. The principal deviations from this standard, as well as the chief points of coincidence with it, it has been my aim to investigate; and although in doing this my attention has frequently been drawn towards various forms of plebeian usage, especially in the matter of declension and the curious mingling of Greek with Latin words, to say nothing of the coining of many odd terms, I feel safe in asserting that in Petronius' treatment of the four prepositions here discussed the Latin language could hardly have been subjected to many very serious injuries.

---

[1] Hist. of Lat. Lit., p. 151.

VITA.

Natus sum Andreas Oliver Secundus Bostoniae, urbis in civitate Massachusettensi, Kalendis Novembris anno Domini MDCCCLXIX, patre Edwardo, medicinae doctore, matre Susanna e gente Mason, quorum alteram adhuc superstitem esse laetor, patrem jam ante hos V annos morte mihi ereptum doleo. Fidei addictus sum evangelicae. Litterarum primitiis in puerorum ludo imbutus, scholam praeceptricis Adam, feminae benigno ingenio et excellenti, per triennium frequentavi; unde auctumno anni MDCCCLXXXI rite dimissus in scholam quae Anglice NOBLE'S CLASSICAL SCHOOL dicta est, cui tum praefuerunt viri excellentissimi Noble, Keith, et Wiswell, transii. Quam cum per V annos frequentassem, deinde uno semestrio propter aetatem meam puerilem in Schola Linguarum BERLITZ peracto, ut linguam Germanicam susciperem, in Universitatem Harvardianam, testimonio maturitatis accepto, almam matrem meam, Cantabrigiae in civitate Massachusettensi collocatam, me contuli, ut inter cives acciperer academicos. Ibi per quadriennium illustrissimos viros audivi, inter alios Lane, Goodwin, Greenough, Shaler, Norton, Allen, Wright, Hill, Palmer, Smith, Royce, White, Sheldon, Grandgent, Morgan, quibus omnibus gratias ago quam maximas; atque anno MDCCCXCI, probatione rite habita, ad gradum Baccalaurei "CUM LAUDE" in Artibus admissus sum. Tum, animo meo ad amorem studiorum philologicorum adverso, per triennium pueros in scholis linguam Graecam, et Latinam, docui, quam plurimam. Mox, autem, amore linguarum ita adductus, ad almam matrem meam ad studia perficienda redii. Ita jam iterum in civitatem academicam per annum adscriptus, ante omnia hoc secutus sum, ut in seminarium philologicum reciperer. Quo impetrato, studia mea sic disposui: primam operam seminario virorum clarissimorum dabam, Allen, White, Smith; eodemque tempore Francisci Babbitt et aliorum benevolentiâ mihi contigit ut societatis philologae sodalibus adscriptus essem. Alteram quandam operam promiscue his viris excellentissimis, Thayer de Novi Testamenti libris, et Hanus de adulescentium disciplina, dabam. Anno MDCCCXCV ad gradum Magistri in Artibus admissus sum; simul item praeceptor in schola quae Anglice POMFRET SCHOOL, in civitate Connecticutensi, dicta est, factus, eo officio per biennium functus sum. Anno sequenti Novum Eboracum bibliothecis utendi causa, aliisque rebus ad eruditionem pertinentibus, ire constitui. Seminarii philologici per haec semestria, Ernest Gottlieb Sihler, Henrico M. Baird, et Frederico Taber Cooper, viris doctissimis et optime de me meritis, studia moderantibus, fui sodalis.

Omnibus quidem quos commemoravi viris gratias et nunc ago et semper habebo maximas. Praematura morte nuper erepti professoris Allen semper servabo memoriam.

Scripsi Novi Eboraci anno MDCCCXCVIII.